Because of She

AF623653

S Karia

BookLeaf Publishing

Presentation by *BookLeaf Publishing*

Web: www.bookleafpub.com

E-mail: info@bookleafpub.com

ISBN: 9789357440523

First edition 2023

DEDICATION

It's all because of She.

So, this is for her.

She knows who she is.

ACKNOWLEDGEMENT

My sister. If it wasn't for your constant need to put me forward for almost everything you think I'm good at in life, this book wouldnt exist.

My baby cub. For endlessly believing in me every step of the way and being my number 1 fan. You will never know how much you mean to me.

She. The one. The only. My everything. Thank you for being my companion in this journey of life. Thank you for finding me. For always finding me. May we always find each other, in all dimensions and all lifetimes. In the here, and the hereafter.

God. The day we realise that people, relationships and everything in this world is temporary, is the day we begin to understand our purpose.

PREFACE

I find that writing poetry is a very private and personal art. I've been writing poetry since I can remember, however never when I am really happy in life. Always when something is missing, when i'm on the cusp of depression or when I'm angry / hurting and full of emotion.

Poetry is like a diary of sorts, as well as a way to channel all that emotion and an outlet for everything bottled up inside, especially if you're an introvert. Hence why most writers are very quiet people, and rarely do poets brag about their latest book publishing to their close friends and family. People they dont know, perhaps, but not people they know. It's almost like inviting them to read your diary, and I dont know anyone, poet or not who would be eager to hand over their deepest most detailed thoughts and prose in their diary, to anyone they know, do you?

Greedy

I want to be loved like they love in the movies,
Or the books i've read.
I want a friend.

Someone I dont have to try hard to fit in with.
Someone who will listen,
And hear my opinion.

About life,
And the universe.

I want someone to hold,
When the nights are cold,
And the bed is a mere casket I lay down in,
To slowly die each night.

I want the stars to dance.
I want too feel as if I'm in a trance.

I want to fall in love with someone,
Who soothes the screaming within me.
Understanding the vulnerable porcupine,
Begging to be held from time to time.

I want to be shown how to shine,
With someone who'll shine a little brighter,

And light the darkest of nights.

I want to be loved by you.

Now.
And always.

Naïve

Like a star,
Feeling the magic of the moon,
For the very first time.

I fell in love.
And you lit up my sky.

Yet how naïve of you to think,
That you were just the moon to me.

You were always,
My whole galaxy.
With the universe in your eyes.

Every kiss from you,
Shining a gentle constellation over my heart,
That only my soul could see.
And only you could touch.

Guide me through the dark days.
And scatter your stars all over me in the dark.

Waves

I dont know what broke first,
My heart.
My mind.

Us.

If only I could love myself,
The way that I love you.
With my entire being.
Through my soul, into my bones.

My love for you is as wild,
And far stretching as the sea.
But you're hell bent on searching the shores.

Do not fear the depths of the ocean.
Just dip your toe in the water,
And let me drown.

I hope as you wander shallow lands,
That in every reflection,
In every window,
Of every bookstore you pass,
You envision me beside you.

Reminding you,
How quickly you turned the pages,
Of our story,
Just so you could get to the end.

And I hope you attract someone,
Who speaks your language.
So you dont spend a lifetime,
Translating your soul.
The way I had.

The Intimacy of Love

Did you see it when I lay in bed,
Careful not to wake you.
Our early sunday morning routines,
Were something I just fell into.

Just waiting for your eyes to open.
Your skin as soft as flowers,
Stealing the morning, our days could wait.
We'd converse for hours and hours.

It's like we never finished our conversations in the evening.
We woke up with a head full of thoughts.
I knew I was no longer asleep nor dreaming,
Had I really hit the jackpot?

I saw it when you'd wait for me,
You'd be standing in the rain.
No matter how long I'd take to catch up,
I never heard you complain.

Did you see it when I would wait for you?
And hold your open coat wide.
While you'd slide your arm into the sleeve,
I'd be holding your bag on mine.

Did you see it when I couldn't sleep,
Unless you'd get in bed.
And let me hook my foot around yours at night,
So I'd just stay up with you instead.

Yes, I saw it when we'd go to sleep,
And you were too damn cold to touch.
So you'd rest your hand on my lower back,
Perhaps I was also your crutch.

Did you see it when I'd smile at you,
Across a room or even a field.
Perhaps I ask whether you saw it or not,
Because I've still not entirely healed.

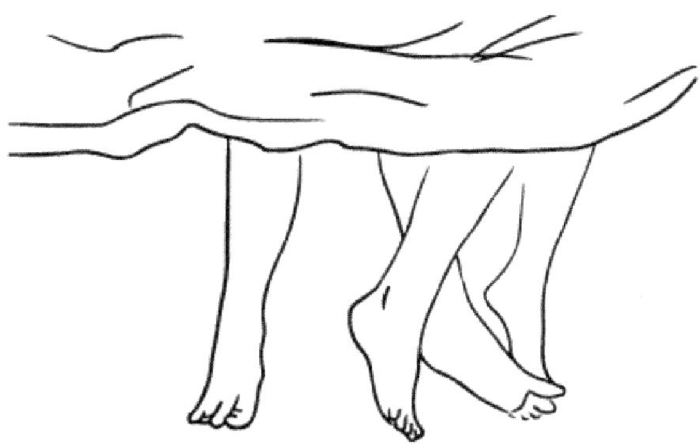

Demons & Dragons

They say love conquers all,
That love always prevails.
Like a magical force that slays dragons,
To get out.

Love never fails.
But I loved her.
And I loved her.

She can't start over.
But if she does,
I hope someone will buy her food,
Not expecting her to eat it.
Knowing about her ever changing diet.

I hope they appreciate the way,
She gets her words wrong,
Or how she refers to everything as 'thingy'.
I hope they dont tell her they dont understand.

I want them to tell her the mole,
The one by her lips, or the one on her neck,
Is the most beautiful spot on her body.
But I hope they dont kiss it.

They'll see the knots in her hair,
And think she's a mess,
But I know she's perfect.
I hope they'll see her that way too.

I hope they don't notice her clothes piled on the chair,
And the way she leaves her socks,
On the living room floor.

What if they pick on her sweaty palms,
The hands I love to hold.
Will they love the scent of her pillow?

I love her.
I dont want anyone elses lips,
Where mine once were.
I dont want any one elses hands,
Where mine are supposed to be.

I dont want anyone else singing to her heart,
Experiencing her new playlist of songs,
Or seeing her at 8am when she's natural,
And looks the most beautiful of any hour in the day.

They won't know where her scars have come from,

Or that crocodiles make her flinch.

I don't want them to notice how she smiles,
When all she wants to do is break down.

They'll assume she's strong,
I don't want them wiping the food,
From the corner of her mouth,
Or pulling back her hair.

That's my girl.
That's my person.

But you can't tell the sun when to rise,
You can't command a flower to bloom.
Nothing natural can be forced into existence.

So, if she has to love someone new,
I hope that someone will be honest.
I hope they appreciate the scars,
Taking their time to touch and feel them.

I hope they read her story,
And feel her in ways that no other human can,
In ways that I never could.

I would have brought her the moon,
When she was in darkness.
I would have brought her the sky.

When she was feeling lost.
And if she ever felt like she needed,
To break apart and fall.
I would have caught her with the whole damn sky.

I hope they love her as much as I do.
As much as I have.
As much as I always will.

Bad Medicine

With all that's left of my heart,
I hope you find the healing & love you are looking for.
We both knew the honeymoon phase wouldn't last forever.
Maybe we didnt want it to.

Maybe we were searching for depth.
Depth that can only be found in low valleys,
After climbing tall mountains together.

I hope you go on long walks,
And drink your favourite tea.
I hope you daydream in music,
And escape this brutal world,
When there is nothing else.

The butterflies of lust need to fade.
For the peace that comes from a medicinal kind of love.
The kind of love that finds your ills,
And gently tends to them.
The medicinal kind of love that heals you,
As much as it inspires you.

I hope, unexpectedly,
Good things come to surprise you.
I hope you go through your day,
Knowing it will be alright.

I hope your heart is held by someone,
Who knows how to hold it.
I hope they never let it go.
I hope this world is kinder to you,
Than it ever was to me.

You taught me a lot.
I know that now.

That deep unconditional type of love,
Cannot exist.
Unless it's been broken.

Roar

Life is beautiful yet brutal too,
A double sided sword.
This journey each of us must face,
To the end we walk toward.
I need you to know, it can be different,
The story is yours to write.
You need'nt hesitate, each step you take,
Girl, you can change your life.
Though demons may have chewed you up,
And spat you out on the floor.
Get right back up and tell yourself,
This will not happen anymore.
No longer will you fall and break,
Your stength cannot be ignored.
You cannot change the world in whisper,
You change it when you ROAR!

Let Me

Let me love you in silence,
A place from where rejection hides.
Let me love you in my lonliness,
Where no one holds you but me.
Let me love you from a distance,
For the void between us may sheild me from pain.
Let me kiss you in the wind,
As the wind is gentler than my lips.
Let me hold you in my dreams,
And may my dreams have no end.

Dark Art

She was art long before I laid eyes on her.
She'll continue to be art long after I lose sight of her.

She's not to be understood.
She is to be felt.

She'll move you in ways that explanatory words could never give justice to.
She'll have you falling,
Thinking you're flying.

Could You?

When you put the textbook definition of anxiety to shame,
I will love you.

With your erratic breaths and quivering limbs,
If you want me to,
I will kiss your lips until you are okay again.

When you begin to isolate and prove that the idealist TV shows and adverts are idiotic and unrealistic expectations of a fantasy world which we do not live in,
And prove over and over again that depression is no field of flowers to sit in,
I will bring you a little light in bouquets of them,
Until the darkness is a little more tolerable.

When you have so much adrenaline in you that you have no clue what to do or why you're excited,
I will put music on and we can have the most amazing dance party.

Through the late night netflix marathons.
Through the therapy sessions.

Through the days you cant decide,
What to wear or whether to change out of your pyjamas.

Through the days you burn your breakfast,
And the days you need take-out for dinner.

When you need a little medication to quiet your mind,
And when you snore so loud that I lose sleep.

When I say it, I mean it.
Through everything.

I will love you.

And so she did.

H2O

You thought she was a drug,
An addiction.

She was your craving,
Your cigarette.

Until you realised, you couldnt quit.
No amount of rehab, nor willpower would help.

No.

She was more than something so addictive.
More than something so toxic.

She was pure.
Necessary.
A requirement to survive.
A part of your whole composition.

She was water.

One Day

And one day,
Your name wont feel like thorns in my mouth.

I will find peace,
In the pieces of me that you didnt pick up.

My smile,
Won't feel like a tiny elastic band forcibly stretched.

I'll sit with people,
Who don't know all about you.
And I'll have no need,
To tell them all about you, just to keep sane.

And one day,
Things will be fair on me.

I'll never think of you again,
Until I close my eyes to kiss.

Dusty Love Letters

Sometimes, it's no longer a heart beat,
It's an ache.

You.

The early morning I always wanted to wake up
to.
The face the sun touches and reflects more than
light,
For the rest of my life.

When you leave,
The moon goes with you,
Leaving nothing but darkness.
Do you think it slips away,
To show how love can travel between souls?

Was our love like dusty love letters?
Unsent.
Lining the basement of our hearts.

Did you creep in and read them?
Keep them.
Each sealed with a piece of my heart,
That will never be whole again.

Perhaps we never stopped loving.
Perhaps we just forgot how to show it.

It will get easier you said.
But no one knows,
If there is life after death.

For the Broken

This is for the days when the person you love the most,
Stops recognising your love.

This is for the ache of unrequited love.

This is for ocean deep love,
And those who are scared of depths.

Your love is different,
And they are scared of taking one more step.

I know.
Your love for them,
Would drown an ocean.
I know.
But they weren't used to a love,
They couldn't contain,
In a droplet.
I hope you make peace with that.

They wont find anyone better than you,
But they will find someone,
Who is better for them,
Than you.

It's heartbreaking,
That after all those promises,
You will be replaced,
And someone else will make them smile.
I'm sorry.

You won't forget them.
Moving on from someone you love,
Is really hard.

You've built all your dreams,
With this person in them.
Left so much,
To be with them.

You wont heal in a snap.
You can't just unlove.
You'll grieve and drown,
In a sea of emotions.

You won't get closure,
It's a scam.

Give yourself time to absorb,
And do away with anything that reminds you of that person.
That shirt that smells like them.
Throw it all out.

All the messages they sent you.
Delete them.

Chose yourself.
Because they didn't.

Be your own hero,
Because you need yourself.
More than you need anyone else.

And, I hope this finds you in time.

Belong

Within this world I dont belong,
The people, the structure,
It's all so wrong.
I cant turn off my feelings so deep,
I can't pretend.
I can't not weep.

I'm just not built like the people I've met.
Dead-set on their greed,
Ignoring those in need.
Trampling and stamping,
On the heads of those,
Who clean their shirts,
And iron their clothes.
I cannot live in dog eat dog culture,
With vultures & coyotes,
It's all just too vulgar.

I need something real,
I need to feel.
No wait. I need others to feel.
As much as I do,
Be sincere, show love,
Don't we all need that break-through?

Equal

You are night,
And I am day.
Ultimately we're,
A living cliché.

You know how they say,
Opposites attract.
It's like we're trying,
To prove it's a fact.

You like the dark,
I like the light.
I sleep in the day,
You game in the night.

But if you look,
Further than you can see.
We aren't so different,
You and Me.
You and I,
Me and you.
I read on the go,
You read on the loo.

You're a diamond,
And I dont quite shine.
Perhaps I am a coal,
A diamond unrefined.
Still we're both carbon,
Atoms and such.
Equally tough,
Yet soft to the touch.

Sometimes it feels like,
We are worlds apart.
Like were such different people,
But with one beating heart.

You can be moody,
An irritating slob.
To which I get angry,
And then act like a knob.

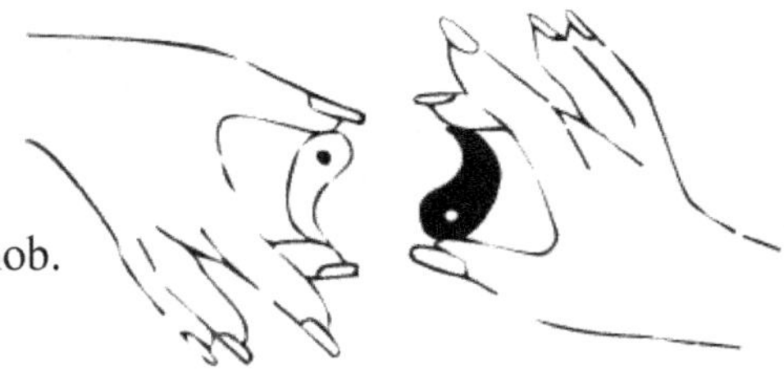

When you are happy,
And touching the sky.
I'm right there with you,
We're both learning to fly.

I don't know whether,
This life has a sequel.
But in this life at least,
I've found my equal.

You Only Die Once

There are times I wish that you were raised,
With me, along by my side.
Just so you could understand what I do,
To understand the religion I hide.

I wish you could have insight & knowledge,
To all that I believe.
So you may perhaps understand me better,
And what in life I hope to achieve.

I was raised to never forget,
That there is life after death.
It's our purpose in life to prepare for it,
From birth to our last breath.

You see I don't believe in reincarnation,
Or that it's as simple as a switch off.
There is a whole eternity just waiting for us,
And it's never too far-off.

What we do in this lifetime,
Determines the quality of the next.
Just be humble and do good,
It's really not too complex.

There is in-depth descriptions,
Of what we can expect.
Reminders we take nothing with us,
But prayers and our respect.

We must try to live a righteous life,
And give generously to those in need.
Don't get too wrapped up in this world,
Blinded by empty material greed.

The aim is to please our creator,
In this life for the next.
Have no physical attachment,
What we have is his to bless.

Be good, be honest, but most of all,
Forget not that he gave you life.
Remember to give thanks and pray in good times,
And not just in times of strife.

This life is a journey, a lesson, a test,
Not all of us will pass.
But we all must sit the same exam,
Against a different sized hourglass.

Every second, every moment,
Each breath we take for granted.
Always be greatful and always trust,
You won't ever be empty-handed.

Don't fall in love with this here world,
It's nothing but temporary.
A dangerous distraction for those of us,
Who ignore the cemetary.

Don't sacrifice the after life,
For a world of evil and sin.
Humble yourself for the love of God,
This world's for shaytan and Jinn.

It's hard I know, this world of ours,
Like drinking salty water.
The more you drink the more you find,
Your thirst just will not falter.

The 'akirah', life after death,
Is more like an endless spring.
To quench your thirst, relieve your pains,
An end to suffering.

Those who are kind, those who believe,
In the streams of milk and honey.
The one's who remember & wish best on others,
The one's who don't worship money.

They're the few who know no one stays,
And help each other pass through.
Through this life, preparing for the next,
No matter what may come, say 'thank you'.

Say, 'Alhamdulillah', and be thankful for,
Everything you've already been given.
Say, 'Inshallah', what will be, will be,
We wake only if God is willing.

'Salaam' means peace, a frequent reminder,
Of how we should behave and interact.
I seldom hear it said anymore,
And it seems harder for me to attract.

'Khuda Hafiz' means, I leave you with God,
A simple prayer said everyday.
I seem to pray a lot less these days,
Am I being lead astray?

There's so much more I can't explain,
In such a short space of time.
I just wish you were raised with the insight I had,
So we'd see the same lifetimes.

Because it's said that when you live & love with this belief.
Then without question.
You can ask for the believer to whom your heart belongs,
To reunite with at gates of heaven.

Less is More

No matter how much I try. I just can't.
I can't get excited by worldly things.
By possesions and jewels,
Or diamond rings.

I just can't get excited,
When a mansion is bought.
Because any house is a home,
With a little love, I was taught.

I'd rather a holiday,
Where I get to spend time.
With those I love,
With lots of cuddle-time.

I hate this world,
Where I have to pretend.
That I love all the fake stuff,
The material trend.

I'd rather just go,
And make someone smile.
Visit a care-home,
To chat for a while.

To spend all my money,
On life's gifted treasures.
Things that cost nothing,
The things you can't measure.

Release me from,
This competitive bubble.
Where we dress to impress,
And we secretly struggle.

I don't need,
For anyone to see.
The 'things' that I have,
From a life of greed.

I'll always be thankful,
For a roof over my head.
Some aren't so fortunate,
Some are already dead.

I really don't need,
More and more.
I just want some peace,
And to visit a bookstore.

I'd rather live daily,
Calm and at peace.
Than keep up appearances,
Until I'm deceased.

So leave me alone,
And let me be.
I may not have much,
But I'm happy at least.

Cub

For you there is nothing,
I would not do.
What ever I am capable of,
It's all for you.

Even that which I can't,
I will find a way.
So don't ever worry,
Mummy's here, okay?

Whatever you need,
At whatever time.
Don't ever hesitate,
You needn't be shy.

I'd walk barefoot,
To Timbuktu.
I'll always be here,
Rooting for you.

You are an amazing kid,
You are truly rare.
Your brain is incredible,
You're my little care bear.

Never forget,
You have my heart.
When I thought life was over,
You helped me restart.

You brighten my mornings,
Just by being you.
My little foodie,
My winnie the pooh.

Just know that I love you,
That will never change.
For now. For ever.
For the rest of my days.

Because of She

Wake up.
Rushed.
Breakfast alone.
No cuddles in bed.

Messy home.
Messy hair.
Messy life.

Laughter.
Pinned to the wall.
Tongues.
Lovemaking.
Not everyday.

Stolen covers at midnight.
Snores.
Slammed doors.

Stubborn disagreements.
Healing hearts.
Forgiveness.
Intimacy.

Coming.

Home.
Love.
Care.

Laughing.
Dirty Laundry.
Unmade beds.

Hard work.
Life.

Swallow the nagging.
Dont say it out loud.
Mute.

Long days.
Easy meals.
Together.
Late.

Emotional.
Breakdown.
Held close.
Cuddles.
Bed.
It's ok.

Believe.
Belief.

Teamwork.

Love is.
Insanity.
Difficult.

It does what it wants.
It will not conform.
To a fairy tale fantasy.
Of how it should be.

But it is worth it.

In spite of.
Because of.
She.

www.ingramcontent.com/pod-product-compliance
Lightning Source LLC
Chambersburg PA
CBHW051738130826
49812CB00033B/914
9789357440523